Al,

We hope you enjoy the book!

Warm Regards,
Steve

Terry
Oct 2018

Ali,
We hope you enjoy
the book!

Warm regards,
Eliot
[signature]
Oct 2015

Endorsements and Praise for *The Pinwheel*:

As a services company challenged by how to improve your offering or a products company, transitioning to a service excellence culture, *The Pinwheel* is a must-read. To get your team on the same page and improve the service culture, everyone from the frontline to the C-suite needs to read this workbook. *The Pinwheel's* great, firsthand, real-world stories, along with the learning associated with the examples, will provide the mortar for the foundation of any customer service–focused organization. *The Pinwheel* is the culmination of Steve and Terry having spent a lifetime developing the tools to transition their organization into one of the most service-centric companies in the world.

—**Christopher Zane**
Founder and CEO, Zane's Cycles and author,
Reinventing the Wheel

While many organizations work tirelessly to align their objectives and measures to an overall strategy, there is often a missing ingredient. Without a service culture, organizations fall short of customer expectations, citing policy and procedures as the obstacles that prevent them from doing the right thing for their customers. A truly customer-centric organization has a service culture at its heart. If this was an easy task, there would be many more examples of companies growing as a result of their terrific customer service. *The Pinwheel* not only challenges us to create that powerful service culture within our organizations but also shows us the steps needed in this journey of continuous improvement.

    —**Adrian Paull**
    Vice president, Honeywell

The power of thanks being a truly cultural enablement to success, it must be included in the vision and belief of any organization. As Steve and Terry tell their stories, simple wisdom comes to the surface for making a strong case for all elements of the Pinwheel.

Steve Church and Terry Cain hit the mark(s)! As they use this metaphor to establish the elements of culture, employee engagement is paramount to ensure success. This framework is easy to audit and begin again when a company has lost focus on what is most important.

    —**Derek Irvine**
    Vice president, client strategy and consulting at Globoforce

As the CEO of a high-growth tech company, I believe that *The Pinwheel* is a much-needed tonic to the usual business book fluff. Terry and Steve's vision of service excellence rings with authenticity.

    —**Max Israel**
    CEO, Customerville

As the President and CEO of a large non-profit, I can think of few priorities more important than plainly defining "Service Culture." Terry Cain and Steve Church clearly identify the fuel that enables

an organization to successfully execute this strategy without exhausting resources, thus ensuring engagement, adoption, and attainment of an organization's objectives.
>—**David Adame**
>CEO, Chicanos Por La Causa

This book is helpful for anyone endeavoring to deliver a great customer experience through values and culture, regardless of whether their business is product, services, or software based.
>—**Lee Benson**
>CEO, Execute to Win (ETW)

The Pinwheel should be required reading for organizations trying to develop a service culture. It asks the right questions and provides a road map to successful transformation.
>—**Ed Petrocelli**
>President, Insight Group

When it comes to customer experience and culture, Terry Cain and Steve Church have a wealth of knowledge. Having been on the practitioner side and the consulting side of building renowned customer experience programs, they can help any organization zero in on weaknesses and turn them into customer experience strengths.
>—**Carine Clark**
>President and CEO, Go Banyan, Inc.

I can't think of a better team than Church and Cain to develop and deliver what is an action-oriented, practical road map for guiding a bottoms-up service culture change in any organization.
—**Steven W. Brown, Ph.D.**
Emeritus Edward Carson Chair and professor of marketing, Distinguished Scholar, Center for Services Leadership, W P Carey School of Business, Arizona State University, and strategic partner, The Insight Group

This book offers invaluable insights from global practitioners of service excellence. A strategic and practical guide with real examples that Steve and Terry implemented themselves at a global enterprise level. Great insights for small and large company alike.
—**Eric Mosley**
CEO and cofounder, Globoforce

With the ever-increasing use of social media and the Internet, the voice of customers has never been stronger. Consumers are no longer held hostage by any one product or company and their "viral" opinion can make or break your organization. Today represents the "Age of the Customer" and every business leader should promote a culture where all employees strive to become a "service hero" as outlined in this book. Terry Cain and Steve Church have shared their incredible experience and insight to clearly demonstrate what it takes to be a service company, and to provide the ultimate customer experience.
—**Kim Taylor**
CEO and president, iPro Tech

The Pinwheel

The Pinwheel

Strategy versus Culture, and the Winner Is …
Improving the Odds in Your Favor

STEVE CHURCH AND TERRY CAIN

THE PINWHEEL
STRATEGY VERSUS CULTURE, AND THE WINNER IS ...
IMPROVING THE ODDS IN YOUR FAVOR

Copyright © 2016 Steve Church and Terry Cain.

All rights reserved. No part of this book may be used or reproduced by any means, graphic, electronic, or mechanical, including photocopying, recording, taping or by any information storage retrieval system without the written permission of the author except in the case of brief quotations embodied in critical articles and reviews.

iUniverse books may be ordered through booksellers or by contacting:

iUniverse
1663 Liberty Drive
Bloomington, IN 47403
www.iuniverse.com
1-800-Authors (1-800-288-4677)

Because of the dynamic nature of the Internet, any web addresses or links contained in this book may have changed since publication and may no longer be valid. The views expressed in this work are solely those of the author and do not necessarily reflect the views of the publisher, and the publisher hereby disclaims any responsibility for them.

Any people depicted in stock imagery provided by Thinkstock are models, and such images are being used for illustrative purposes only. Certain stock imagery © Thinkstock.

ISBN: 978-1-5320-2833-5 (sc)
ISBN: 978-1-5320-2835-9 (hc)
ISBN: 978-1-5320-2834-2 (e)

Library of Congress Control Number: 2017912428

Print information available on the last page.

iUniverse rev. date: 10/28/2017

Steve is dedicating our book to my wonderful adult children, Kimberly, Jessica, and Daniel. They have taught me the true meaning of patience, perseverance, and unconditional love. Through them I've learned that as a parent we don't have to be perfect, we just have to love.

Terry is dedicating our book to my sweet Becky, my constant source of inspiration, and to Jon and Katie, the new Cains to challenge the world!

CONTENTS

Foreword xiii
Introduction xix

Chapter 1	The Jerry McGuire Effect—Show Me the Money: Virtuous or Factual?.............................1
Chapter 2	Inspiring the Dream: Vision 9
Chapter 3	Do All Employees Live the Core Values? Integrity/Values 15
Chapter 4	To Serve or Not to Serve: Attitude 19
Chapter 5	Think in the Customer's Shoes: A Ritz-Carlton Story 25
Chapter 6	Eat or Be Eaten: Culture Adaptability 29
Chapter 7	I Did Not Steal Your Cow Today: Knowledge and Skills 35
Chapter 8	Are Your Systems and Processes Customer Centric? Systems/Processes 41
Chapter 9	Do as I Say, Not as I Do: Accountability 45

Chapter 10	Without the Secret Ingredient, This Tastes Terrible: Passion	51
Chapter 11	To Lead or Not to Lead: A Message to Senior Leaders	55
Chapter 12	Speaking of Adapting and Changing, Are You Ready for Millennials? You Better Get to Know Them	63

Summary 69
Key Points 71
Closing 77
About The Authors 79
Endnotes 83
Acknowledgments 87

FOREWORD

Right now, my personal favorite company is Amazon—a company with a culture of service excellence and deep commitment to customer centricity. I, like many people today, rely on Amazon for just about everything I might need to purchase or shop for—if not for the actual purchase, certainly for shopping, browsing, and comparing items before I purchase. I am never disappointed. The service I get from Amazon is remarkable in terms of convenience, information, speed, reliability, and customization. A quick story. I was on the phone with my mother (over ninety years old) one evening, and she was looking for a specific book for her book club. She had gone to the library but found herself number 300 on the waiting list for the book. So while we were talking, I looked up the book on Amazon and told her I could buy it for her for nine dollars.

"Great price," she said, "but then you would need to package it and mail it to me."

"Not at all," I said. "I can just have it sent to you directly, and you'll have it in two days."

She was amazed! So for nine dollars and some odd cents, I bought the book and had it sent to her. Of course, it arrived on time at her doorstep.

Service excellence, as demonstrated in this story, is appreciated and valued by customers and easy to recognize. Its absence is even

THE PINWHEEL

easier to observe, and, unfortunately, its absence is often more memorable. Adding to this story, I can attest that Amazon clearly has a strong culture of service excellence in the way that Terry Cain and Steve Church describe it in this book. They are deeply committed to customers (even a customer obsession), innovation, and (very important) long-term results because sometimes being innovative and doing the right thing for customers is not immediately profitable.

Successfully sustaining a culture that can deliver excellent and consistent service day after day is challenging for most organizations. This is particularly true for organizations that haven't grown up with a culture of service and customer focus—such as the Amazons, Disneys, Southwest Airlines, and Starbucks of the world. Often, these companies want to move quickly toward this type of culture because they are convinced of the benefits of doing so. The benefits to companies of having a service culture are proven—increased employee engagement and loyalty, increased customer satisfaction and repeat business, greater share of wallet for the firm, and ultimately greater profitability. Yet getting from here to there presents a daunting task for many organizations. This is especially true in the modern-day business environment where so much is changing all the time, customers are more involved, social media is a constant player in the mix, there are strong pressures to reduce costs, and employees want purpose and meaning in their jobs. The Pinwheel and its elements are a great way to get started on the journey toward a service culture, and it is a great framework to return to as the environment and people change.

FOREWORD

I have known Terry Cain and Steve Church for a very long time through their association with Arizona State University and their involvement with our Center for Services Leadership. They are students of service and leaders and creators in the service world. They have regularly spoken to executives in our programs, and they have presented their ideas in my MBA class on service marketing and management year after year, receiving rave reviews from these diverse audiences. Why? Because they speak from the heart, they love teaching through stories, they have strong and concrete examples, and they are proven leaders with a passion for what they do. They also speak the language of business and the language of execution because they have done it themselves and can speak with authority about what really works, how it works, and why it is important.

Through the Pinwheel framework, Steve Church and Terry Cain share their personal stories and their life experiences working at Avnet in pursuit of a culture of service excellence.

What they say is true. It is indeed some of the very foundational values, attitudes, and beliefs that can create a culture of service and sustain it. Keeping a focus on these fundamentals and reinforcing them through leadership, words, and actions are keys to success. Clearly, Jeff Bezos, CEO of Amazon, and his employees and customers know this to be the case.

My favorite definition of service culture is one that comes from the early 1990s and is still as relevant today as it was then.

THE PINWHEEL

> A Service Culture is a culture where an appreciation for good service exists, and where giving good service to internal as well as ultimate, external customers is considered a natural way of life and one of the most important norms by everyone. (Christian Gronroos, 1990, 2007)

This is a very rich definition that has many implications. First, an "appreciation for good service" must exist. This does not mean that service is the flavor of the month or a program, but rather, that service is appreciated and valued consistently over time across the organization. The second part of the definition stresses that good service is given to "internal as well as external customers." In other words, employees deserve good service, too, and serving them well is an essential requirement for, in turn, serving the ultimate customer. Finally, giving good service is also viewed as a "natural way of life" and something that is important to everyone. As times change and challenges arise, service remains a core value and natural way of life.

To sustain this type of a service excellence culture requires attention to many things. Steve and Terry have captured these many things succinctly through their Pinwheel and related stories that bring its elements to life. What they share in this book and in their talks and workshops is not only relevant to pure service businesses but also any business (B2C, B2B, large, or small) that wants to build and sustain a culture of service excellence. Both have decades of experience working in the heart of the business, building employee engagement, customer focus, and customer experience strategies, frameworks, and models to transform the organization. You have much to learn from their experiences, examples, and stories.

So turn the page, and begin to unlock the secrets of a service excellence and customer-focused culture. You won't be disappointed.

Mary Jo Bitner, professor and co–executive director,
Center for Services Leadership, Arizona State University

UNKNOWN RUMOR MONGER

"Now that Amazon has announced its purchase of Whole Foods, Americans are excited and pushing Jeff Bezos to buy the US Post Office, the entire health care system, and United Airlines!"

INTRODUCTION

A friend served in a local church as a pastor for a number of years. After losing touch with him for a while, we discovered that he had left the ministry and is now a manager of a successful Starbucks store. As we caught up on life, we were impressed by his comments about how much he loves his job and the culture of his new employer. He had some interesting thoughts about how people are actually treated better and with more value and respect than they might be in a church environment.

Interesting, isn't it? That an institution (a church) that believes in expressing love, joy, peace, and treating one another with compassion would measure poorly in comparison to a corporate culture like Starbucks?

To quote management thinker Douglas Smith, we have discovered "that our churches, schools, and neighborhoods no longer define our values. Instead, corporations do. Unfortunately, they're not usually up to the task."[1]

Churches are institutions and as such are organizations that employ people, some paid and some volunteer. The result of this is that churches have cultures like any other organization. But the priority and value of a person seems to be the new spiritual ground of corporate America. We hear terms like "human capital" working toward "total rewards" (both terms are Steve's personal

THE PINWHEEL

least favorites, as to him it sounds like we have relegated humans to statistics on a balance sheet).

The fact is that companies like Southwest Airlines and Starbucks seem to get this notion that all service and productivity is derived from the engagement of their employees.

We have been on a journey together. A journey of observing the service levels provided by many, many companies with a particular focus on what is behind the service that is being delivered. How much of it is systems and processes, attitude, leaders who are leading by example, and many other factors. As we became managers, leaders, mentors, and teachers, we developed a keener understanding of what true excellence in customer service looks like. The lessons were everywhere, available to us as we set foot in a place of business and observed how we felt, were treated, and were honored (or dishonored) as customers. One of the great aspects of studying customer service is that we are all in a lab every day as customers. We observe and experience everything from the best to the worst. And we continue to ask the question, is the customer experience improving, staying the same, or going backward?

Every November at hotels like the Ritz-Carlton or other fine hotels in Phoenix, Arizona, an event known as the Services Symposium is held. Arizona State University's Center for Services Leadership hosts the event. In essence, it is a celebration and sharing of ideas and best practices focused on great customer service, services, and solutions. There cannot be a better place to hold this event than the Ritz-Carlton, a brand that reminds us of what creating a great customer experience looks and feels like.

INTRODUCTION

When we attended this event for the first time, all our passion for customer service began to grow as we heard story after story of cultures that were, at that time, unconventional in business. As we heard, and later taught, the concepts of the service-profit chain resonated with other believers within our company regarding how value is created in our businesses. Introducing the service-profit chain at Avnet was a major breakthrough, and it helped our executives understand the relationship between engaged employees, the creation of loyal customers, and the realization of what all companies seek—that is, shareholder value creation.

We are excited to take you along with us on a short journey. Certainly, you can challenge almost anything we offer in the pages that follow. But you won't get a chance to do it until you take the challenge yourself and prove or disprove what works in your organization.

Why Did We Write This Book?

Good question. Since writing takes a lot of time, we would only undertake this project if we believed we had something important to say. (Otherwise, we could have worked on our golf handicaps.) We all know that there is no shortage of material available in print or online about customer service. We had to ask ourselves whether there is anything unique that would cause the reader to finish the last page and think, *That was worth the time, and now I need to put these concepts into action.* Our answer to that question was an obvious and enthusiastic yes. Why? Because we strongly believe that any change, including a journey to customer experience excellence, must be consistent and friendly to the culture of the company. It's estimated that something like 85 percent of all consulting agreements fail, and in the majority of these cases, it is because the change is at odds with the culture of the company. The employees, being somewhat passive-aggressive, nod and voice some agreement and then head for the watercooler, where they discuss how they are not going to support the change. So what's unique about this book is that we attempt to share insights into how you can successfully implement customer-centric behaviors into your employees because there is compatibility between those behaviors and, "how we do things around here," our working definition of culture.

To summarize, we wrote this book for the following reasons.

First of all, we believe that great customer service is a key differentiator as it is one of the few ways a company can beat their competitors and grow profitably. By the way, you probably have a great opportunity if you get moving quickly as great customer service is still rare in most industries. We don't have to tell you that. Like us, you are all customers and experience the same frustrations we do in our daily lives. And we normally don't ask for all that much, right? Just give us what we asked for, provide us with reasonable value, treat us with a little dignity and respect, fix the problem quickly if you make a mistake, and we are happy.

Second, in most companies, great customer service is typically delivered by a group of what we call "heroes." These are the people who just get it, as though it is in their DNA to exceed their commitments every time. They take pride in creating great customer experiences. Although this is admirable, it won't allow

INTRODUCTION

your company to deliver great customer service on a consistent basis, every time, every day. And if you want your name, your brand, to be known as the great customer service company in your competitive arena, you need more. What is more? The "more" is that you need to create a *culture* of customer service excellence, where every employee understands the importance of great customer service, and every employee understands their role in delivering it.

> **"No one person can totally satisfy a customer ... but any one person can totally dissatisfy a customer!"** [2]

In other words, all of the great services delivered by your heroes can be undermined by one person who doesn't share the vision.

Our Gift to You

As avid readers, we are irritated by business books that insist on being three hundred pages long. We're sure publishers encourage this, as though a belief has emerged that the thickness of a book determines its value. What happened to the concept of the value of our time? We have a different view; only offer what is relevant and will make a difference—no more, no less. So this is not your typical fifty pages of value, 250 pages of fluff book. We value your time (and ours), and the quicker you finish the last page, the quicker you can get on with application.

How to Use This Book

This book is intended to guide your management team(s) in creating a culture of service excellence.

At the end of each chapter is a section titled "Questions for Engagement and Action." These can be used in a standalone fashion with your team to focus on one of the attributes of creating this culture. In this way, each business owner or leader can adapt the specific topics in order to fit the needs of his or her business. Since the content of each chapter is simple and requires little need for preparation, they can be pulled out again and again for use during process evaluation or to drive continuous improvement. This is important because as your strategies change, you will need to make sure your service delivery can support it. And no matter how fast you move, when your competitors realize that you are beating them through great service, you will need a plan to move faster! Our hope is that every one of these topics will help you to create the kind of culture that will truly differentiate your business in your respective marketplace. At the end of the day, your people, your culture, and your processes will be the key differentiators in your arena. It is of paramount importance that you enable the people in your business to create lasting value and customer engagement like only they can.

INTRODUCTION

What Is the Pinwheel Metaphor?

Remember the pinwheel, that colorful childhood toy that spins on the wind? Most of us remember it as a fun diversion, but maybe it is more.

What do pinwheels do? They catch the wind. They show the visible movement as the consistent shape of each vane of the wheel retains movement and speed. Each vane has the same value and catches the same wind, and it spins the wheel round and round. If one or two vanes are damaged or of a different size, the wheel slows down. If one wheel vane were huge, there would be surges of movement at intervals, and the whole effort would look jerky with inconsistent movement and speed.

Sound familiar? We are not talking about wind but about unpredictable market conditions—beliefs, economy, culture, competition—that influence businesses. We're not talking about a toy but a collection of vanes that twirl together to ensure consistency and growth. Each element, or vane, in this book is story based and can be emphasized differently at different times.

These elements, like the pinwheel, catch the winds of the marketplace and if applied consistently, will drive profitable growth and allow employees to flourish and possess a sense of pride in their company. And one of our biggest learnings is that the best changes occur when they are driven by the employees. This can and does happen when the culture of the company promotes it.

At Pinwheel Partners, we do not have all the answers, but we think we have some of the right questions. Our role is to coach, guide, and inspire your business journey and help with just a little bit of fun along the way!

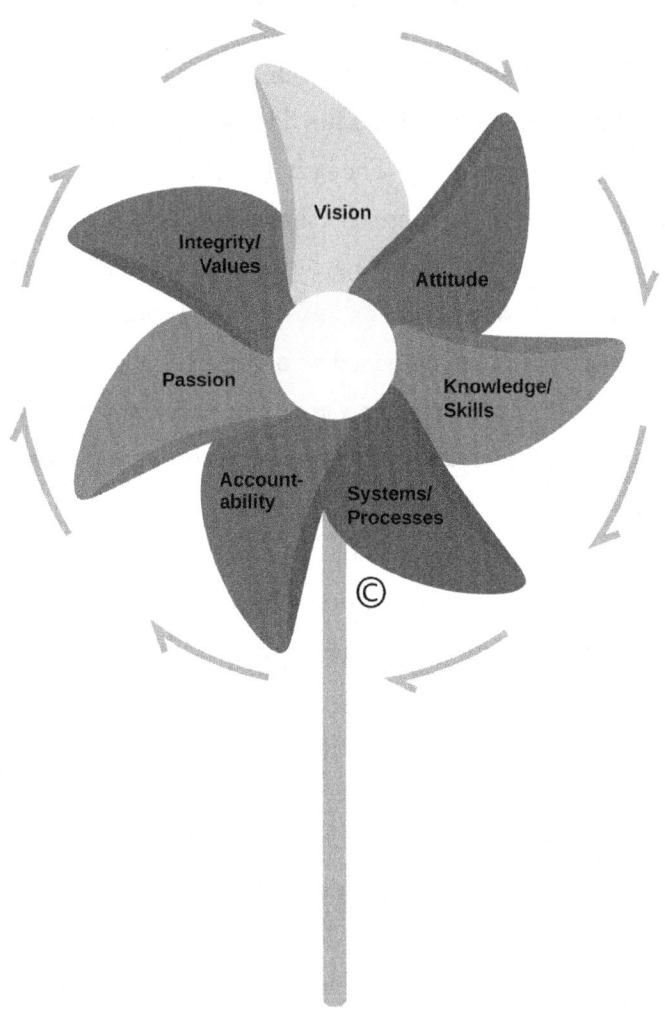

Used and adapted with permission from Avnet, Inc.'s "Wheel of Service Excellence," originally created by Terry Cain and Steve Church, copyright Avnet, Inc., 2007. All rights reserved.

CHAPTER 1

THE JERRY MCGUIRE EFFECT—SHOW ME THE MONEY: VIRTUOUS OR FACTUAL?

Our experiences in observing and studying various types of customer service delivery have taught us that people fall into two categories. There are those managers/institutions that believe the effort of meeting or exceeding customer commitments is virtuous and that it should be done because, well, it's the right thing to do.

Others, however, will need to see tangible proof that great customer service will make their companies more profitable.

Although we believe both camps can benefit from reading this chapter, it's really designed for those who need to see the proof. As Jack Webb used to say on *Dragnet*, "Just the facts, ma'am."

Growth to Maturity

Many of the examples we use come from the high-technology industry. However, it's our guess that they will apply in many, if not all, other industries. In the high-technology industry, one where we have spent our entire careers, we have watched the industry

THE PINWHEEL

move from growth to maturity. What does this mean? It means that products become commoditized, price pressure exists, and it becomes more and more difficult to differentiate a company's value propositions and, as a result, get paid commensurately. At this point in the life cycle of your industry, you should be asking, "In what ways can we differentiate our company and beat our competitors?" One of the few answers might be the most obvious but is often overlooked—deliver better service than any of your competitors.

To help you determine if your industry has moved from growth to maturity, we offer these attributes[3] of maturing industries.

1. Declining gross profit margins
2. Slower top line growth
3. Ongoing industry consolidation
4. Fundamental value propositions challenged

Sound like your industry?

Three Questions

As the president of Avnet's largest business for many years, Steve made it a habit to visit customers whenever he was in a market. He always asked customers these three questions to get the conversation started.

1. Why do you buy from my company?
2. Why do you buy from my competitors?
3. What could I do to earn more of your business?

As an introvert, this worked well for him as he not only got the answers but didn't have to worry about breaking the ice, something introverts are typically not good at. More to the point, the big epiphany for him was that the answers always focused on service.

As a supplier, we often tend to think in terms of products, quality, price, the competency of our sales team, and so on. Although those things carry some weight, in the customer's mind, they pale in comparison to doing what we say we will do, every time. And "Tell me when you are going to have a problem, so I can plan for it." And "If you have a service failure, show me you care by fixing it immediately." We have a strong suspicion that if you asked your customers those three questions, you will get similar responses.

Let us pose this as a question: Do you believe your company is responding to what your customers want and need, or are you doing what you *think* they want and need? Or just be honest; you don't have much of a clue, but you are doing what you believe will make the most profit for your company.

Primary Value Is Shifting

In our industry (high-technology distribution), the primary reason our customers purchase from us has changed. Many years ago, it was product based; that is, we had the products they needed at a competitive price. But as products became commoditized in our maturing industry, we could no longer differentiate on price or availability. Our competitors had the same products and offered them at basically the same prices. At that point, the purchasing decision became related to the services we provided along with the product. Today, more and more, it's about the solutions we provide that address the customers' problems that make *them* more competitive and allow *them* to meet or exceed *their* customers' needs. Does this sound familiar to you as you think about the challenges your company is facing?

An Epiphany

Another question for you: Is your company attempting to move from being a products company to a services and solutions company? If so, here's something you need to accept. Your customers are not going to trust your company with complex services and solutions if you cannot do the basic things right. If you are not meeting or exceeding your commitments on the simple things your customers ask you to do every day, why would they trust you with more complex services and solutions that can cripple their businesses if you fail?

Stop Shrinking

In his book, *Double Digit Growth*, Michael Treacy lists the five sources of revenue growth. Guess what the first one is—base retention. To grow, you first have to stop shrinking. His point is that as companies build their growth strategies, they typically miss an important point; they are losing customers. As customers leave your firm, you actually have to grow more than you anticipated to make up for the lost revenue from existing customers. Does your company have a process by which you can identify customers who are leaving? Can your company identify customers who are thinking of leaving? More important, do you know *why* customers leave your firm, and are you taking the appropriate measures to keep others from leaving for the same reasons?

Good—and Bad—News Travels Fast

It used to be that if your company delivered poor customer service, the only people who knew were your customers. Not anymore. Today, with the Internet and social media tools like blogs, wikis, Yelp, and YouTube, poor service becomes public knowledge. Your brand and reputation can become tarnished with customers you have never even done business with.

The positive or negative value of your brand directly correlates to the time, effort, and attention given to the quality of your customer service culture. And these attributes, for example, can be measured by Net Promoter Score (NPS) or Client Lifetime Value.

> **Questions for Engagement and Action**
>
> 1. Do the leaders in your company meet with a sufficient number of your customers to truly understand how well you are meeting their needs? Are they asking questions like these?
>
>   - Why do you buy from my company?
>   - Why do you buy from my competitors?
>   - What could I do to earn more of your business?
>
> 2. Do your customers believe you are in this for relationships or just transactions? How do you know?
>
> 3. Do you have a churn report? Are you tracking how many customers are leaving your firm and how many you are gaining with regularity? We suggest quarterly reviews at a minimum.
>
> 4. Do you have metrics/data on customer complaints?

A Note on Building Consensus

We thought it would be a good idea to talk about consensus. Some of you, as you read this book, might be wondering, *Why not just decide what we are going to do to improve the customer experience and then mandate it?* You could certainly do that. However, we believe there are a couple of reasons why you don't want to.

First, people support what they help create. This is called inclusion, and it is very important. Towers Watson, Gallup, and others all agree that as few as 32 percent of today's employees are engaged in their work, leaving the rest of the population as not engaged, or worse, disengaged in their jobs. People kill what they don't help create. We call the disengaged employees *"disrupters"* because they not only dig in their heels, but they attempt to spread negativity inside the company as well. How can this be acceptable in a culture?

> **Disrupters are a personality type. If that's the case, get them out of the way of people trying to do their jobs. They're poison.**
>
> Jack Welch

Second, you might think it will take less time to mandate, but our experience says it might well take you longer. You see, the job or transformation is not finished when you roll out the mandates because whatever you decided has to be implemented by your employees. Because they weren't involved—and may not even understand the why, how, when, and who of what you mandate—it can easily take a very long time to get to implementation. Our process involves including all of a company's employees in building its culture of service excellence. By educating and including all of the company's employees, it might take longer to get to implementation. But implementation itself will take far less time. In the end, our experience says you can get through implementation faster and with much less pain by asking your employees to be actively involved in building the service culture.

> **The soft stuff is the hard stuff.**
>
> Dr. Michael Hammer

CHAPTER 2

INSPIRING THE DREAM: VISION

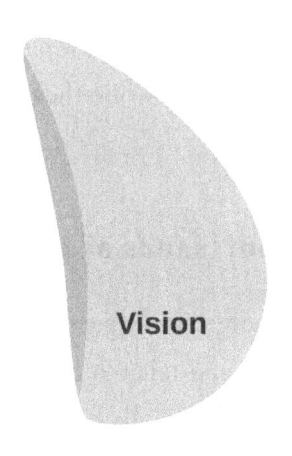

Vision

Before we get started in defining this culture of customer service, we need to understand some things. Things such as what and how vision actually occurs, how necessary it is, how to create it again and again, and how ultimately to bring clarity to it over and over. This is not for the purpose of building a vision statement, which most companies and many departments have adopted, although it may inspire you to do so. This is a workbook, a process to actually help you create a tangible description of what it will be like when you have reached your goals of building a customer service culture. You will be tempted to be very tactical here. You should play with lots of verbs in the description, and again, stay away from trying to build a plan on how to get there. A plan has the purpose of establishing the how, and that will come up in a later chapter.

Our definition of "vision": a dream with a deadline, typically three to five years in the future.

What do you think your vision is for a customer service culture? What images does it conjure up in your mind as it relates to your business or your department? What behaviors will create it? What do customers feel like while they are experiencing your products or services?

Hands of a Surgeon: Hands of a Salesman

There is the story of the surgeon who goes into third world countries, finds kids in classrooms, and talks to them with enthusiasm and passion. At one point during his talk, he would hold a child's hands in his hands, proceed to examine them closely and sincerely, and then enthusiastically proclaim, "These are the hands of a surgeon!" To another, he would dutifully examine his or her hands and exclaim, "These are the hands of a nurse!" or "These are the hands of a teacher!" or some other role. This doctor was inspirational and gifted in giving many children a gift or a vision of what they might become, of what they could aspire to be, and of who they might help in their future. He does this by touching hands and

VISION

proclaiming a message of hope or inspiration and placing a new and wonderful image in a child's mind. Something very similar happened to Terry in his early days at Avnet.

I had been working for Hamilton Avnet for only a few months in 1974 when I had the opportunity to meet the CEO of our Fortune 500 company. At first, I did not know the significance of this meeting but later learned why we had reached this prestigious position in the marketplace. As with some other companies, ours was one in which the leader embodied the culture and values that defined us. At this point, I am proud to add that this company had achieved an emotional position with many of its suppliers, customers, and employees. That is, there was a human element that drove people to want to do business with us, to be connected with us. Tony Hamilton came back into the ten-thousand-square-foot warehouse on the south side of Phoenix, Arizona. He had about forty-five locations like this at the time, four hundred employees in all, and $450 million in annual revenue.

Although I was working in the warehouse, Tony Hamilton took the time to reach out to meet me as well as each individual in the warehouse. He did this to ensure we understood our importance and our future. He said to me at that first meeting, "Terry, you are a salesman for our company!" This surprised me. I had met some salesmen and knew that they were smart, respected, knowledgeable, and well compensated. This was far from the image I had of myself, or what I thought I could be. I was content to be a warehouseman and happy to have the job I had!

I politely asked Tony, "What do you mean?"

Tony said, "Terry, you see, there are engineers who come in

this back door each day to pick up small quantities of parts for their projects. They are building products of some kind. They are inventors. These inventors build their dreams in their basements, garages, and living rooms and will keep doing this until their dreams become realities. One of these days, you will be helping someone who will invent something important, something that will be needed by many people. They will sell their ideas, and instead of purchasing small quantities of parts from us, they will purchase in large volumes."

Well, needless to say, I had a new perspective on how important my lowly warehouse job was! I was a representative of my new friend, Tony Hamilton, who believed in me, believed in the customer's needs, and wanted to serve those needs. (One of Tony's innovative practices was that for many years, he established no minimum order so that these entrepreneurial engineers would have a company to purchase from that was easy to do business with. After all, he foresaw that these engineers could become part of something significant someday.)

Well, Tony was prophetic, at least in Phoenix anyway, and I'm sure in other warehouses around the country. A man named Marty Wilcox came to the back door of our Phoenix warehouse, where I was working, at least weekly, sometimes daily, to pick up his parts. Sometimes it was as much as a few hundred dollars, but many times, his request was under a hundred dollars. I think the last time I saw him at our will-call window his order was fifty-seven dollars and change. Yes, we even had to make change from the petty cash just for those who came to will call and were not on an open account. At that time, Marty said to me that he

VISION

probably would not see me again. I was a little alarmed, since he and his twelve-year-old daughter had been a weekly conversation for several months by then. He replied, "Yes, we are starting a company with this product I invented. We will still buy parts from Hamilton, but the volumes will be too large to pick up here at will call. You will be shipping them in large boxes, like those over there." He pointed to boxes getting ready for the UPS man, all with our standard yellow-and-black tape so you couldn't miss them in the receiving dock!

You see, Marty invented a machine now known as the ultrasound and began a large company in Phoenix. This firm bought millions of dollars of parts from Avnet for many years. Later, I heard that Marty had left the company after a large medical manufacturer acquired them, and there were several million reasons he had for leaving.

Was I inspired by what Tony had said to me months earlier? Did he put the importance of a vision in my head that helped my belief system engage with our customers in a way that hopefully made them all want to do business with us? Did they sense my wonder and curiosity about what they were building? Was there anything I did that helped them realize their dreams? Probably not, but I was realizing a dream each day in the process as I believed I was a salesman, making a difference to Tony Hamilton. The rest of my story is yes, I became a sales leader in our company too.

So you are running a business, department, or project. What are you saying or doing to inspire those around you? What visions are in their minds that they are working toward that you helped place there? Is it just enough for them to rise to the occasion and

13

be a true believer in what you said to them, or, better yet, do you challenge them to create a part of that vision on their own and make it even better and brighter from their points of view? Or think back to the surgeon. Can you help your employees see a vision for themselves and their careers that goes beyond what they might be seeing today and can inspire them to reach heights they haven't considered? How will you spend time with them? What will you say?

Questions for Engagement and Action: Vision

1. What will you do to inspire and create a vision for customer service excellence in your business?

2. Is your vision for creating customers down to every level of employee?

3. Are all customers treated with the same courtesy, respect, and attention, or are some just forgotten?

Some Pointers

* Focus on vision and ideas that create vision.
* Think about what Tony did for Terry.
* Think about what the surgeon did for those children.
* Think about the strengths your employees have, and write down some statements or questions that will help them rise toward a united specific vision.
* If you are an individual contributor, apply these questions to yourself and your job.

CHAPTER 3

DO ALL EMPLOYEES LIVE THE CORE VALUES? INTEGRITY/VALUES

Integrity/Values

Now that you have a picture in mind regarding how you want to serve your customers and what their experiences will feel like to them, we begin to identify the how and what to meet this new culture we are building.

Businesses all have a set of values, written or implied. If you have identified values, you have a great start. If your values are well understood by your employees, you are more than halfway there on this one. But if you have identified core values and your leaders do not follow them, they are in fact meaningless and work against the culture you are trying to create.

THE PINWHEEL

The Liar

When I (Terry) was about twenty-seven years old, I was the general sales manager of our local branch. I was leading a group of field salespeople who were all older and ostensibly wiser than I was. It is very likely that I was arrogant, proud, and full of the importance of all that we were accomplishing and the goals of our business unit. I had only been married for about six months. What follows is a conversation I remember very clearly as it was one of those "crystal moments," when someone was holding me accountable for something. I feel certain it did not go as smoothly as I will relate it to you.

As I arrived home from work one night, my young, beautiful wife looked me in the eye and said, "You are a liar!"

"What do mean? A liar? Come on!" I was proud of my integrity, my character, and my sense of honesty about how I conducted myself, so this came as a complete surprise to me.

She went on to explain. "You say you will be home by 6:00 p.m., and you show up at 7:00 p.m. Or you say you will be home at 7:00 p.m., and you show up at 7:30 p.m. You say one thing and do something else. This makes you a liar."

I explained, "You don't understand. I start leaving the office, and someone stops me and needs to speak to me. And then another employee is in the parking lot and needs to talk. It is just part of business." I was really on thin ice here. I did think I was right for a while, but then my conscience taught me something. The fact was that I did say one thing, and I did something else; that is indeed a lie. Okay, I was a liar, but I could do something about it. We did get it right after that, and I became pretty good at honoring this important commitment each day.

So let's swing this thought around to how we deal with our customers. Are we liars? Let's say a customer who we've done business with for a long time asks us to have our proposal to them by 2:00 p.m. We have every intention of meeting the commitment. We arrive only about five minutes late. Nothing is said about it, so it should be okay, right? Do you think your customer remembered? Let's say it happens again. This time we are ten minutes late, and still nothing is said. Hey, we were old business partners, right? No big deal. But trust in relationships is fragile, and if you are not moving in a positive direction in building a relationship, it is going in the opposite direction.

So here is the tough part. A competitor made the same commitment, 2:00 p.m. He arrived at 1:55 p.m., and suddenly my failure to make good on my commitment is revealed. As a result, there is an exposed difference in what someone else did and in what I did. I did not do what I said I was going to do.

In my defense, our business is based on the efforts of many people in the process, and we are dependent on many others for their help to meet our deadlines. But we are responsible for keeping our word *every single time*. Our customers do not expect us to be perfect, do they? What they do expect is for us to commit to integrity and simply do what we say we are going to do. (We are big fans of Stephen Covey's book *Speed of Trust*. His research identifies thirteen competencies that equate to how integrity is won or lost.) This has to be applied to internal customers as well as external customers because it is the only way the enterprise can really serve the customer.

Values may seem like mere words, but they do mean something when you hire and fire to them. This sends a message regarding the culture. It also focuses you and your leaders on the work of making decisions and builds consistency of behavior all around. Therefore, values make a safe place to work for everyone at every level. Now, of course the optimum culture is a performance- and values-based one. Most companies understand the performance basis, but they cannot compete without the values system. You must have both.

Questions for Engagement and Action: Integrity/Values

1. What do we mean by values? Let's use your words.

2. In your company, are your values well understood by all employees? Are they real? That is, are employees, especially leaders, living by them? Do you hire and fire to your values?

3. Do your employees have a say in creating the core values?

Note: Do you have corporate or company values to live by, or are they just plaques on the wall?

CHAPTER 4

TO SERVE OR NOT TO SERVE: ATTITUDE

Attitude

Uncle Ben's Quote Book, by Benjamin R. Dejong, was on my (Terry) desk each year as a young manager. I was impressed by quotes from Abraham Lincoln and so many others. The guy named Anonymous seemed to inspire me the most. One of those quotes, "Attitude is 90% of achievement," kept after me for years.

But how can we prove this?

Attitudes are more important than facts.

Dr. Karl Menninger

ATTITUDE

Let's discuss how we actually impact others with attitudes. Pine and Gilmore's book from 1999, *The Experience Economy*, was leading edge thought leadership when they predicted that in the future, businesses will compete on "customer experience." They used Disneyland, the "Happiest Place on Earth," as an example. Woe to us! How can we create Disneyland-like experiences in our businesses? We don't have Cinderella and Mickey Mouse to spread happiness and joy. So in our companies, who creates the customer experience? What kind of employees? Happy, enthused, engaged employees who put their hearts (attitudes) on the line with every customer encounter develop and sustain that experience.

So maybe there's hope for us who don't offer Fantasy Land, Tomorrow Land, Adventure Land, and Frontier Land. But how would we do that? Back to the question of who creates the customer experience. People! Okay, so what causes our people to deliver a great customer experience?

The answer is that we need to engage our employees to the highest degree possible. Engaged employees feel valued and respected, trust and believe in senior management, have a good and open relationship with their bosses, and have the tools and training to do their jobs. They will go the extra mile because they want to, and they are also our best recruiters.

And how do we engage our employees? Through open and honest communication, by listening to them, by making sure we practice meritocracy (most deserving person gets the monetary reward, promotion, or recognition), by earning their trust, and by investing in their development and careers. That doesn't seem that hard, does it? Except that research indicates a different picture; over 20 percent of employees in most companies are *actively disengaged.* We refer to them as disrupters because they are actually working against the company. And fewer than 20 percent of the employees are *actively engaged.* Between 55 percent and 60 percent are *neutral,* meaning that they are stuck in the middle, not actively going out of their way to either help or hinder the company.

So if you and your company really want to deliver a great and consistent customer experience, you need to invest in driving high levels of employee engagement.

Employee engagement can create the wind that spins the pinwheel faster, meaning a virtuous cycle that inspires growth for the whole culture.

Conversely, a few missteps from leadership, like saying one thing and doing another, slow everything. Steve used to say, "A real leader can never have a bad day." By that we mean employees are watching and need the assurance that everything is fine; there is no cause for concern. Being fully present in your workplace is critical as the employees derive comfort and confidence by watching their leaders and taking cues from them. A leader could have a personal problem or just have come from a meeting where there were unresolved conflicts he or she is wrestling with. Walking down the hall, avoiding eye contact, not engaging or encouraging the team is a formula for an anxious, scared, disengaged workplace. The employee only has a few choices when this happens. If given to insecurity (who isn't from time to time?), he or she wonders, *What have I done, and will I be let go soon?* Remember: this is simply a leader walking down a hallway one day. If it is repeated regularly, the end is near because the second choice is for the employee to leave on his or her own. Employees are strong and know there are leaders who care about people out there, and life is just too short not to enjoy your work and believe in the people you work with!

> **Questions for Engagement and Action: Attitude**
>
> 1. How important is it for leaders to act and communicate positively every day? Do leaders set a tone for the organization by their moods and behaviors?
>
> 2. Do leaders understand they are in a fishbowl every day, and employees watch them carefully to take cues on how the company is doing?
>
> 3. If leaders are having a bad day, what can be done to avoid sending negative signals?

HAPPY EMPLOYEES

Dave Ridley of Southwest Airlines once said, "If you want happy employees, hire happy people."

CHAPTER 5

THINK IN THE CUSTOMER'S SHOES: A RITZ-CARLTON STORY

My (Terry's) first experience at a senior leadership conference was in Amelia Island, Florida, at the Ritz-Carlton Hotel. This is an incredible location with a great hotel, like all the Ritz properties. An extraordinary experience happened to me while at this resort.

Similar to many conferences, our daily schedule included events running late into the evening and then we started first thing the next morning. There were always planned team builders so that fun was part of the conference. Usually there was a group of us who would plan for a tennis match late in the evening or very early in the morning, before the start of a new day. This event was no exception. There are beautiful clay courts there; a very different tennis experience. As one who lettered in the sport in high school and played one season of college matches, this was a treat for me at that time in my early thirties.

The slower play and the anticipation of sliding across the clay surface of the court were pretty intriguing. But I digress. Actually, not really. This lets you know I was a little disappointed

THE PINWHEEL

when a match needed to be canceled because a partner in doubles did not have access to a tennis racquet. So it's now 11:00 p.m., and I call the operator to leave a message for my colleague, Bob Braverman (this is before cell phones, to date myself). It is late, so I just asked the operator to leave a message. Here is how our dialogue played out.

> Me: Hello, this is Terry Cain in room 143. I would like to leave a message for Bob Braverman, another guest in the hotel.
>
> Operator: Sure, Mr. Cain. What is your message?
>
> Me: Thanks. Please tell Mr. Braverman that we will not be playing tennis in the morning as I could not get another tennis racquet.
>
> Operator: Mr. Cain, I can get a tennis racquet for Mr. Braverman.
>
> Me: Thanks, but you don't understand. Our business meeting starts at 8:00 a.m., your pro shop opens at 9:00 a.m., and our plan was to play at 6:00 a.m.
>
> Operator: Mr. Cain, I will have the night watchman open the pro shop to get the racquet and then meet Mr. Braverman on the tennis court at 6:00 a.m.

Now, my expectation was that the operator's job was to deliver a message. That would have been perfectly fine in this case; all I expected was for her to close the loop on our potential plans. But instead, this employee understood her corporate mission and believed she could do something to remedy my situation, even though I did not ask her. This is how great customer service is created. The operator looked beyond my request, which was to leave a message. She focused on providing a solution to the real problem, which was that I needed a tennis racquet. This is the type of service companies can unleash when they have engaged employees who understand the mission of their companies.

We like to talk with our classes for a few minutes about the motto of the Ritz-Carlton: "We are Ladies and Gentlemen serving Ladies and Gentlemen."

Wow! What a powerful message is conveyed in a few words. We ask our classes these questions.

1. What does this say about the employees of the Ritz-Carlton, regardless of their job titles or positions?
2. What is the role of every Ritz-Carlton employee?
3. What does this say about the customers who stay at the Ritz-Carlton Hotels?

Back to our story. What happened here with Terry, Bob, and the operator?

The rest of the story is what you might expect, plus a little bit more because you will see the discretionary effort of another employee. The night watchman entered the scene.

The night watchman must have realized that it would be dark at 6:00 a.m. that time of year, so he went to the pro shop, retrieved the tennis racket, and met Mr. Braverman at 5:45 a.m. to escort

THE PINWHEEL

him in the dark with his flashlight, so Bob would have no trouble joining us at the courts for a little fun before work.

Why is this story so incredible? It is incredible because these employees were empowered to think in the customer's shoes. How do we teach every employee to consider these unexpressed wishes? Is this an attitude or a skill?

The hospitality business may be easier to brainstorm because the product is hospitality or service to people who come to be served in a given setting. In actuality, though, any industry services people. And any of us can think in the customer's shoes for our mutual benefit, especially if leadership has modeled it for us.

Questions for Engagement and Action:
A Ritz-Carlton Story

1. What are some of the customer wishes in your industry?

2. How will you reward or recognize employees when they meet or exceed unexpressed wishes?

3. Are employees given freedom to serve their customers and empowered to solve problems without management involvement?

4. What are the best reminders for keeping this spirit alive in your business?

CHAPTER 6

EAT OR BE EATEN: CULTURE ADAPTABILITY

Building a business that rises to prominence is challenging. However, we have observed that staying at the top is possibly even more challenging.

One of the reasons is that it is easy to fall victim to paradigms. What are paradigms? They are models or patterns of something, an example or a standard.

Let us give you a couple of examples. The Swiss owned the wristwatch market for many years with a very high share of the market. Their standard was the Swiss movement watch. That was their paradigm of what a watch should be, and their success was based on it. However, companies that were not stuck in the paradigm of the Swiss movement watch saw a different way. Enter the digital watch. The Swiss watch industry's share of the global watch market dropped dramatically and has never recovered.

In the 1980s and into the 1990s, Motorola gained a large share of the cellular phone industry with the analog phone. They rode the success of their technology, but the problem is that we tend to get stuck in our paradigms, and it's difficult to see another way. Along came companies like Nokia and Ericsson with digital phones; they were not invested in the paradigm of the analog phone. Motorola's share of the cellular phone market dropped precipitously. Again, they never recovered their lost share of the market.

But wait—while the digital cellular phone manufacturers were invested in the digital phone because that's how they became successful, along came Apple with a smartphone. And we all know what happened next. What is our point? Simply that when our success has been based on doing things one way, it's hard to see beyond that paradigm to another way. Just look at Apple versus Samsung.

Both of us are big Starbucks fans. In fact, we suspect that their success, which is well documented, could in part be attributed to our patronage. Okay, that could be a bit hyperbolic.

One of the things we do in our workshops is to ask classes to name the companies they consider to be great service companies, those that deliver consistently great experiences. One of the companies that is usually mentioned is Starbucks. We ask the classes to tell us what it is about Starbucks that they love. As we record their answers, here are the most typical responses.

> I can get my drink the way I want it.
> They remember my name.
> It's a great place to meet friends or hold a casual meeting.
> If they mess up my order (rare), I get my drink for free.

And the one that doesn't come up, but we suspect would if people were being honest—it is a place to see and be seen. What's interesting is that at least in our classes, no one ever mentions the quality of the products, although we wouldn't go there if they weren't good.

Starbucks really created a new category through an amazing service experience. Not only that, but they have continued to innovate in many ways. Is their future safe and secure as a viable and profitable enterprise? Is there a challenger?

We live in the Phoenix, Arizona, area. Steve currently owns a home in Idaho because that's where his grandchildren are. He doesn't want to miss any opportunities to spoil them rotten, much to the chagrin of their parents!

This is where Steve was first introduced to Dutch Brothers coffee. Like Starbucks, this is another amazing company. Founded in Grants Pass, Oregon, in 1992, what started as a single location is now well over two hundred. The company is privately owned by two brothers, Dane and Travis Boersma.

So why do people go to Dutch Brothers? Steve thinks there is a simple answer—because it's fun. It is a great and fun service experience. Is the product they sell of high quality? Yes, it is very good. But what sets them apart is the attitude of the employees, an attitude that translates into fun for the customer. They have also made an improvement in the drive-up window category since in most locations, you can drive through on either side of the coffee hut. Steve loves this because you don't have to drive around the block if you happen to enter on the wrong side of the drive-through.

Like Southwest Airlines before them, the Boersma brothers set out to provide a great experience for their employees as the number one priority. Herb Kelleher, the head of Southwest Airlines for twenty years, was considered a heretic when he said it's a company's responsibility to look after the employees first.

> **Your employees come first. And if you treat your employees right, guess what? Your customers come back, and that makes your shareholders happy. Start with employees and the rest follows from that.**
>
> Herb Kelleher

But trying to catch and pass the category leader doesn't always work. Does anyone remember Ted or Song? These were attempts by United Airlines (Ted) and Delta Airlines (Song) to go after a different slice of the market, one dominated by Southwest Airlines. They both targeted lower-cost leisure travel from 2003 to 2006. Though marketed profusely, they were unsuccessful against Southwest's preeminence.[4]

Why weren't they successful? Could it have been culture? Herb Kelleher said, "You don't hire for skills, you hire for attitude. You can always teach skills." PetSmart took a similar approach when they began to offer pet grooming. Their first approach was to hire experienced groomers. However, as a company that must compete on service to be successful, they decided to go in a different direction by hiring employees who loved animals and were service oriented. Then they taught them the skills of grooming.

One thing is for sure. No matter how well your company is doing today, you will need to protect and grow your position by innovating. And in doing so, you will need to guard against getting stuck in what made you successful. Paradigms are powerful, and history reminds us that they can cause us to miss seeing a new and better future. The essence of this book is about culture. It's noteworthy that culture is the most powerful resource any company has, and it is either an asset or a liability. As Peter Drucker is attributed to have said, "Culture eats strategy for breakfast."[5] Culture has the ability to prevent change and inhibit innovation, and the result is that this can cause product categories or companies to die. Innovation can only come from leaders who consistently make it safe to fail and learn, and fail and learn, and fail and learn.

Questions for Engagement and Action: Adaptability

1. Discuss how employees would answer this question: Is it safe to fail around here?

2. On a scale of 1–10, is your cultural essence more like Southwest, as a 10, or like many motor vehicle divisions, on the low end?

3. Is there clarity on the why we do what we do for all employees?

4. How hard is it for a frontline employee to make a change to please a customer?

CHAPTER 7

I DID NOT STEAL YOUR COW TODAY: KNOWLEDGE AND SKILLS

Knowledge/ Skills

Okay, we all know that our customers must be made aware of the products and services we offer in order to thoughtfully determine if they want to partake of them. We can build this awareness via marketing programs, sales calls, brand recognition, or best yet, through word-of-mouth referrals. The basic skills in a customer service culture must be there, communication skills being among the most important. After all, if we are not hearing the customer needs correctly, we cannot deliver the appropriate set of products and services. We are going to provide you with a fun and impactful lesson in this chapter that will prove to you the

THE PINWHEEL

power of nonverbal communication. As a result, you will discover that texting, e-mail, and social media methods of communicating are risky when communicating important information.

It has been our observation that one of the critical components of delivering great and consistent customer experiences is listening skills. It is also one of the most overlooked areas for skill building.

When we were kids, how many times did we experience the forced, "I'm sorry," to a friend, a sibling, the dog or cat, or even directly to our parents? I (Terry) remember it like it was yesterday. It goes like this.

> Say you are sorry, young man!

Head down or eyes diverted elsewhere, a whimpered, sarcastic "I'm sorry," comes out with a little more volume than expected. I remember stubbornly standing there forever, saying what I thought Dad wanted to hear, yet he would not let me budge! After all, I was saying the words. But you get it, right? Communicating meaning is very little about the words alone. The words are necessary, but they must be consistent with body language and voice inflection.

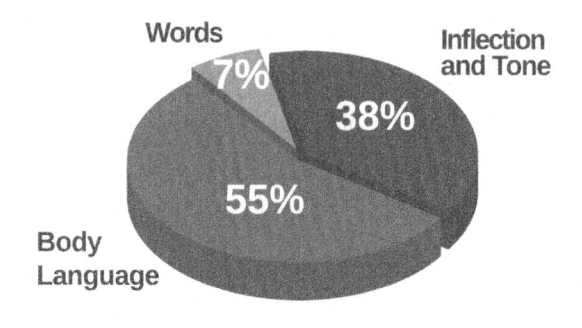

Pie chart: Words 7%, Inflection and Tone 38%, Body Language 55%

Based on research by Albert Mehrabian, Ph.D., Professor Emeritus, UCLA. See his book *Silent Messages*.

Most of how we make connections with customers is a communication of some sort—that is, voice, in person, web, e-mail, and so on. These are all ways we connect with a desire to communicate in a full dialogue with our customers. It seems that how we communicate is still a frontier, but there are references that can help us understand what may not yet be intuitive for some of our employees.

There is a Harvard study that references the need for positive feedback.

> Only positive feedback can motivate people to continue doing what they're doing well, and do it with more vigor, determination, and creativity.[6]

Other research indicates that it takes six positives to overcome one negative comment.

> The study, done by the University of Michigan Business School several years ago, compared team performance to the frequency of praise and criticism given within the teams.
>
> The best-performing teams used about six times as many positive comments for every negative one. It found that the worst-performing teams, on average, used three negative comments for every positive one.[7]

It seems to us that it requires a great deal of emotional intelligence for managers to encourage and affirm their employees

THE PINWHEEL

while pointing out areas for improvement in the proper balance. But that's a topic for another book!

> ## Questions for Engagement and Action: Knowledge and Skills
>
> So now that we understand this, please have some fun and complete this exercise. You will be glad you did, and you might have a shot at changing your culture when your teams really apply these principles.
>
> 1, Type or write on paper seven times, "I did not steal your cow today."
> 2, In the first iteration, underline the first word. "I did not steal your cow today."
> 3. Underline the second word in the second iteration, the third word in the third iteration, and so on.

4. Cut each of these seven sentences into strips, and fold each strip in half.
5. Randomly disperse the seven strips among the group.
6. Now, have each person stand up and read his or her strip aloud with great emphasis on the underlined word.

<u>I</u> did not steal your cow today.
I <u>did</u> not steal your cow today.
I did <u>not</u> steal your cow today.
I did not <u>steal</u> your cow today.
I did not steal <u>your</u> cow today.
I did not steal your <u>cow</u> today.
I did not steal your cow <u>today</u>.

7. After each one is read, the facilitator asks, "What could that have meant?" Group discussion ensues.

Note: This is one of Steve's favorite exercises. You can see the lights go on in the class as the students realize that by simply emphasizing a different word each time the sentence is read, the entire meaning of the statement is changed. Not only do they start to realize how important voice inflection and tone are to the meaning of a sentence, they also start to think about how dangerous e-mails, texts, and so on can be when body language and voice inflection/tone are absent.

CHAPTER 8

ARE YOUR SYSTEMS AND PROCESSES CUSTOMER CENTRIC? SYSTEMS/PROCESSES

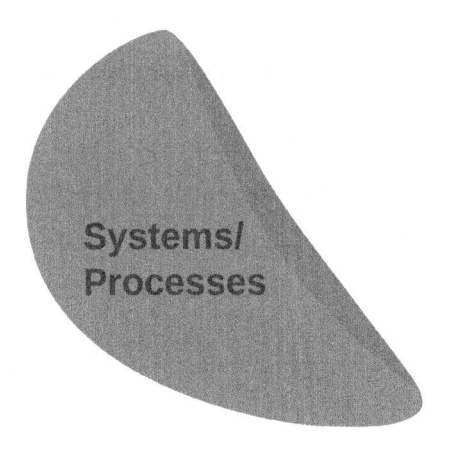

Systems/ Processes

Great customer experiences can be viewed as a combination of attitude, systems and processes, and policies. We have already established the fact that of the three of these, attitude is the most important. As we like to say, poor systems and processes coupled with great attitudes of service on the part of your employees can still translate into great service. However, excellent systems and processes coupled with poor attitudes of service will often result in poor experiences for your customers.

So why did we add a chapter on systems and processes? Were we just trying to make the book thicker? No, that's not why. It's because good systems and processes designed with the customer in mind, or outside in, free your employees to deliver great service experiences. Even your employees with the best service attitudes can get bogged down in broken processes and poor systems, to the point where they can't manifest their desires to serve. So in the optimum environment, you have designed systems and processes that serve the customer and serve the employee, therefore allowing great service attitudes to thrive.

How Systems and Processes Enable Great Service

Some years ago, during high season in Phoenix, meaning the weather was good and the snowbirds were here, I (Steve) called one of my favorite seafood restaurants on a Saturday night to make a dinner reservation. The background is that my wife decided at the last minute that she wanted to go out to dinner instead of cooking, which is, of course, her prerogative. Undaunted, I called this restaurant because we had on multiple occasions experienced great food and service, not only at the Phoenix location, but also at their restaurant in Irvine, California. Calling to get in, however, turned out to be a bit of a challenge because I was attempting to make a reservation on a Saturday night at 7:00 p.m. during peak season.

My phone call was answered by a pleasant woman who asked

SYSTEMS/PROCESSES

how she could help me. I told her that I realized it was a bit late in the game, but I wanted to make a reservation for dinner at 7:00 or 7:30 p.m., only a few hours away. She courteously explained to me that they were very busy, but she could get me in at about 8:45 p.m., maybe 9:00 p.m. I was disappointed but understood that my request was somewhat unreasonable. I explained to her that those times were too late, and I would look elsewhere. As I was about to hang up, she said, "Pardon me, but could you give me your phone number?" I complied, and she said, "Mr. Church, I see that you attend our restaurant often, and we want to thank you for your business. If you would like to come to the restaurant and be seated in our bar area, we will find a table for you as soon as possible."

My wife and I did just that, and within about ten to fifteen minutes, we were seated and had another enjoyable meal.

Let's examine what happened. First, I called this particular restaurant because we had had several great experiences in two of their locations. In other words, they were building customer equity with me. This means that every time I had a good experience, my positive experiences went into a bank account. This is important because what if I went to the restaurant now and had a bad experience? Would I decide to never go back? No, because there is lots of equity in the account. It would mean that I would take a withdrawal against the account, but it would not come close to affecting my loyalty.

Second, similar to the Ritz-Carlton story, the server, in this case the hostess, endeavored to solve my real problem, which was that we wanted to eat dinner at the restaurant within a certain

43

time window, and she was willing to go the extra mile to make that happen.

> **Questions for Engagement and Action: Systems and Processes**
>
> 1. What systems and processes did this particular restaurant have that enabled a great customer experience?
>
> 2. What systems and processes does your company have that enable a great customer experience?
>
> 3. What systems and processes could you add that would enable a better customer experience?
>
> 4. How important was attitude in this story?

CHAPTER 9

DO AS I SAY, NOT AS I DO: ACCOUNTABILITY

Account-
ability

Service Failures Are Inevitable—How Your Company Responds Makes All the Difference

One of the most neglected but critical components of great customer service is service recovery. Try as any company might, there will still be times when you will let your customer down. You ship the wrong parts to the wrong location, you bill incorrectly, or you may add value to the product, but in some fashion do it incorrectly, and so on. When you fail your customer, what do you do about it? Do you stop everything to make it right and show how much you care, or do you put it on the back burner until you can get to it later?

Now, we always like to say, "Don't prove this by purposely failing your customers." Believe us—it will happen on its own. When it does, what will you do?

Here's a story about great service recovery, or accountability, that demonstrates the power of making things right.

Some years ago, I (Steve) was staying at the Hotel del Coronado in San Diego. For any of you who have stayed there, it is a beautiful, historic hotel in one of the most gorgeous spots anywhere. I was attending a meeting of our executive board and board of directors. Once a year, we meet with the board to spend a day on the strategic direction of the company. Then some additional meetings with the board are held.

As I was the first presenter for the full-day strategy discussion, I wanted to get over to the meeting room early to make sure everything was set up properly. On the way over, I stopped at a coffee bar that was in the shopping village on the Hotel del Coronado property. I ordered my usual, a chai tea latte. And as I like my hot drinks hot and knew I would be busy with the meeting room, I ordered it extra hot.

I was the only customer in the coffee bar, and the young woman took my order, although with little enthusiasm. When she handed me the chai tea, I decided to taste it before I left to make sure it was extra hot. What I didn't realize was that she had

ACCOUNTABILITY

not snapped the top all the way onto the cup, so as I took a sip, the top came off. The hot drink spilled down my bottom lip and chin and onto the front of my clothes. Oh, and I found it had definitely been made extra hot!

Well, what was the response from the server? She handed me the dirty towel she was wiping the counter with so that I could dry myself off. No apology. And she didn't even offer to make me another drink for free!

So I have several problems at this point. First, I have a quickly reddening chin from burns, and my clothes are toast. Additionally, I now need to go back to my room and change, which I realize will eat up all the time I had allocated to getting to the meeting room early and ensuring a proper setup. And last, I realized that I would be out of shirts shortly, as I did not plan to wear a shirt for just fifteen minutes that morning.

So back to the room I go, and all along the way, I am thinking that I will never return to this hotel. By the way, I never considered whether or not the coffee bar was part of the Hotel del Coronado or separate. I didn't care. This is a good lesson for those of us who provide products or services to our customers that we purchased from someone else. This is quite relevant for our company as we are a distributor. When you let your customers down, they don't care whether it is your company or something you are providing from someone else. If they placed the order with you, you are responsible. So face it and be accountable.

Back to my story. I changed into my last shirt and headed back to the board meeting. When I arrived, the CEO's assistant asked why my chin was red and blistered. I shared the experience I had at the coffee bar but truly was not thinking anything beyond simply answering a question.

When I arrived back at my room at the end of the day, I noticed a gift-wrapped box and a card on the table. The card was from the general manager and said,

> Mr. Church, I am aware of the experience you had at the coffee bar this morning, and I want to sincerely apologize on behalf of the Hotel del Coronado. The coffee bar is an independent business, but it does not matter. We, and I, take personal responsibility for the unfortunate and I understand painful experience you had to start off your day. I want you to know that we have discussed this incident with the employee and believe we have fixed the problem. Please accept this shirt from the Hotel del Coronado as a token of our apology. If the size is wrong, or for whatever reason you would like to exchange it, please feel free to do so in our Logo Shop. Sincerely, the General Manager.

Okay, so how do you think I am feeling about the Hotel del Coronado at this point? At this point, my thinking changed from *I will never come back*, to *Hey, this hotel really cares about me, and I will return*. Yes, my entire position changed as a result of great service recovery. In fact, I am more loyal to the hotel now than I was before the tea incident, not to mention how many people I told this story to! By the way, research says that we are five to ten times more likely to share our bad customer experiences than our good ones,[8] so just imagine how many people would have heard my bad story if not for the general manager.

So is this the end of the story? Not quite. The next morning, as I was preparing to check out of my hotel room, I received a call from the general manager. She said, "Mr. Church, again, I want to apologize for what happened yesterday. Is there anything else I can do to make this completely right with you?" Needless to say, I was completely blown away by this phone call and could think of nothing else to request.

Questions for Engagement and Action: Accountability

1. Does your company have a service recovery process? If so, describe it.

2. If not, what steps would you take to build one, what would it look like, and what would it feel like to the customer?

3. How are you currently holding yourself and members of your team accountable for delivering excellent customer service?

CHAPTER 10

WITHOUT THE SECRET INGREDIENT, THIS TASTES TERRIBLE: PASSION

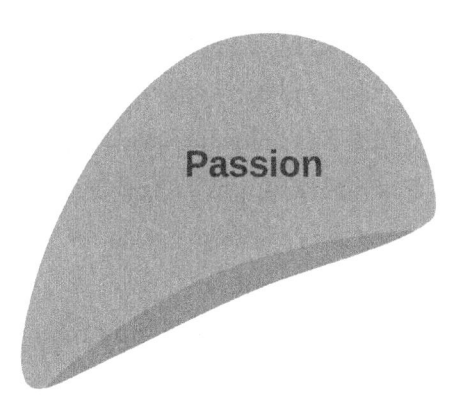

Passion

The stories in previous chapters are just a few examples of our personal experiences. We think that you likely have similar stories and can understand and resonate with all of them. We hope you will replicate them in some form for your own cultures.

We have noodled on prioritizing these elements of a culture of service and came up short. All the elements must be present, and all will need to be continually refreshed and improved on. Also, remember that we are talking about culture, so your reward and recognition systems, as well as your hiring practices, will need to reinforce each vane of the Pinwheel.

If we were to choose one element, passion would be the one we consider mandatory. Without an underpinning of passion in all these efforts, creativity is stifled, and consistent forward motion wanes. There has to be a breakthrough of belief for this to happen.

Lately, we have gone to the Internet and used YouTube as a library of inspirational short videos that establish the same type of passion.

To start with a negative example, check out "United Breaks Guitars."[9] Wow, this is a demonstration of passion, and not the kind you want. This series of songs, like the rage study, emphasize the cost of poor service and a customer's revenge. Not only has this band developed a cult following (with more than seventeen million views), Harvard Business School has published a case study and quantified profit loss in excess of $100 million for United Airlines.[10] This loss was all because leadership did not listen or believe service recovery was important.

The following three examples are all indicative of positive passion that started virtuous cycles and can also touch us as human beings.

To start, you need to watch *Johnny the Bagger*.[11] Johnny is a nineteen-year-old bagboy at a local grocery store who has Down syndrome. Johnny, because of his passion, brought about a transformational change to an entire grocery chain. It's a simple story with a simple message, and in turn, it offers hope for each of us to apply our beliefs and hearts (passion).

Likewise, the popular movie *Facing the Giants* gives a great example of a coach's passion, inspiring his team's leader to drive winning performance. The clip we have in mind is titled "The Death Crawl" scene from *Facing the Giants*.[12]

We can even find inspiration from a child. Our favorite illustration of passion is a young boy learning to ride his bike for the first time and offering his enthusiasm to the world. This is a must-see. It's only one minute long, so please watch this one if nothing else: *Thumbs Up for Rock and Roll!*[13]

Questions for Engagement and Action: Passion

After watching one or all of the videos, have your team talk about observations of the videos.

1. Do you see similar examples of passion in your own business?

2. Why? Is it consistent? Are leaders demonstrating passion as it relates to the success of your employees or your customers?

CHAPTER 11

TO LEAD OR NOT TO LEAD: A MESSAGE TO SENIOR LEADERS

We want to make sure we include a chapter specifically devoted to senior leaders. Why? Quite simply because without your full knowledge and support, there is no point in taking the first step.

The first meeting we want to have when we meet with a company to discuss employee engagement, customer experience, building a healthy culture, or change management is with senior management. We need to present what we do and then help senior management determine whether they are prepared to support their employees in bringing about true change. In other words, are they willing to support cultural change? Your employees already know what needs to be done; they are just waiting for you to get in the boat with them. Give them permission to build something great.

If you don't believe having an engaged workforce matters, don't start down the road to building one. Why would you want to build up the hopes of your people if you aren't committed to seeing it through? If you don't believe engaged employees, with empowerment, are capable of designing a great and consistent customer experience, you shouldn't start. The only thing worse than doing nothing is to do something and then not see it through.

Are you willing to lead by example? It's one thing to make speeches and write letters to employees, and it's altogether another thing to be out in front. As the saying goes, the way to be a leader is to find a parade and get out in front of it. There is a parade happening within the ranks of the employees all the time, and it's in advance or retreat.

Are you willing to conduct employee surveys, listen to the things employees are saying that need to be changed, and make those changes? And then to conduct a survey on a regular basis, every year or two, committed to making continuous improvements?

Are you willing to meet with customers yourself, ensure that customers are one of the main topics in your staff meetings, measure customer experience via a regular feedback process, and make improving the experience a priority? It's a simple process: ask, listen, understand, and act. However, we also understand that you have many priorities, including financial performance. Do you believe that having an engaged workforce and delivering a consistently great customer experience translate into improved financial performance? If you do, let's get started.

Here's a very simple assessment you can do to determine where your priorities lie.

List the top three priorities that your company is focused on today.

Did employees make the list? How about customers? If your list does not include employees and customers but rather financial performance, operational metrics, asset management, product innovation, and so on, ask your team how you will achieve these metrics without engaged employees and customers.

Looking at customer focus, we have observed an interesting phenomenon. In most startups, the owners are extremely focused on customers as they are their lifelines. Serving their customers is the highest priority because without customers, they have no business. The greater challenge occurs as the business grows, and these owners need to hire employees. They may notice that the new employees just don't care as much as they do about customers, and the service level typically diminishes. The challenge for small businesses centers around hiring new employees who care for customers as much as the founders do.

In larger companies, we see a major focus on customers at the frontline level. However, in moving up the hierarchy to higher levels of management, there is a decreasing focus. Part of this is understandable, of course, as managers, directors, and vice presidents don't interact with customers on a daily basis. However, our observation is that it's too easy for managers and executives to distance themselves from customers and become detached. The problem is that these are the people who are allocating the company's precious resources, and they are doing so without understanding the needs of their most important stakeholders, employees and customers. And by the time you get to the senior level of many companies, executives rarely meet with customers, and staff agendas rarely include much mention of customers. So the question becomes, *How do medium and large companies prioritize customers when they aren't on the priority list?*

THE PINWHEEL

Years ago, when teaching classes to employees in our company, we would ask the students, who were all managers in our company, how they believed our company ranked employees, customers, suppliers, and shareholders. (Note: As a distributor, suppliers were an important component of our success.)

Without fail, every class (average class size ten) would answer this way:

1. Shareholders
2. Suppliers
3. Customers
4. Employees

We would then ask them if they were comfortable with this ranking, or if they thought it should be changed. Again, without fail, the classes would reprioritize the list as follows:

1. Employees
2. Customers
3. Suppliers
4. Shareholders

When we asked them why, their thought process went something like this.

Engaged employees will deliver a great customer experience. When customers buy more, suppliers get what they want. When all of this happens, shareholders get what they want. To quote Jack Welch,

There are only three measurements that tell you nearly everything you need to know about your organization's overall performance: employee engagement, customer satisfaction, and cash flow.[14]

We agree with this sequence and believe that employees of your company know what needs to be done. They might not know precisely how, and they may not have the tools and training they need today for success, and they might not have been empowered to affect change, but that's where you and your management team come in.

Frontline employees want to serve customers. When you provide them with the tools, training, and incentives to do so, you are not only improving the customer experience, you are also building employee engagement. Why? Because you are helping your employees succeed, to do what they want, to serve customers. Okay, you may have some employees who don't really care, but if they can't get behind this, you really don't want them anyway.

Change Management

Yes, what we are talking about involves true change and a change management process. Starting with you. Why? Because companies don't change; people do. In other words, change happens in a company one employee at a time. Yes, there is a tipping point at which the majority of employees get on board. But it starts with you and your senior team.

We have seen examples where change occurs at the grassroots level in companies, but without senior management support. The

THE PINWHEEL

result is that a great deal of pressure builds up in the system. And as a biologist by education, I (Steve) know that pressure in the system eventually needs an outlet.

We are students and believers in the Prosci Change Management Process and their acronym ADKAR.[15]

A—Awareness. Employees need to be made aware of the fact that a change is coming.

D—Desire. True desire needs to be created in the employees. They need to want to be part of the change because it makes sense to them.

K—Knowledge. Employees need to have the knowledge required to be part of the change process.

A—Ability. Employees need to have the skills required to do their parts.

R—Reinforcement. The change process needs to be reinforced regularly, through communications, rewards and recognition, success stories, and especially by senior leaders leading by example.

ADKAR is not linear; it is in fact circular. It doesn't start with awareness and end with reinforcement. After reinforcement, it starts back at the beginning. And it's like a pinwheel. That is, done right and consistently, it builds speed and momentum.

We are often asked about the difference between knowledge and ability. Think of it this way. You can watch videos and listen to instructors to learn how to play golf. You have the knowledge, but that does not mean you have the ability. You golfers know that well!

By the way, the ADKAR model works beautifully in other areas of life as well. As an example, I (Steve) wish I had this knowledge when I was raising my children. My style, much to the chagrin of my kids, was to announce a change and expect that they were on board. However, I failed to explain why the change was necessary (awareness), get them in the boat (desire), provide them with the knowledge and ability to change, and reinforce the change through incentives and encouragement. Being a parent would have been so much easier had I known about ADKAR. Nevertheless, I have three grandchildren now, so, ADKAR, here we come!

In summary, your employees watch your every move to try to understand what is important in your company. What are your priorities? Not what you say they are, but what you demonstrate by your actions. If you desire an engaged workforce, a consistently great customer experience, and a healthy and resilient culture, you will have to make those things a priority in everything you and your senior management team do.

Questions for Engagement and Action: Senior Leaders

1. Is there transparency between leaders and subordinates?

2. Is there a change management methodology that works in your business?

3. If it works, great! If not, is there a belief that knowing how your company can adapt and change is worth embedding in the culture? If yes, move on to the next question.

4. If how we change is a belief and a core value, how can you make it a part of the culture linked into the strategy and vision?

CHAPTER 12

SPEAKING OF ADAPTING AND CHANGING, ARE YOU READY FOR MILLENNIALS? YOU BETTER GET TO KNOW THEM

We thought we were finished writing this book, but then we realized that with the millennials entering the workforce in significant numbers, a few thoughts about them is merited.

The Millennial Employee

In 2016, Gallop, Inc., published an interesting study, "How Millennials Want to Work and Live."[16] Consider these facts and how they pertain to your business.

According to Time.com, by 2025, three out of every four workers globally will be millennials.[17] Why not start building your company culture to appeal to millennials now, since it's going that way anyway?

Eighty-nine percent of millennials would prefer to choose when and where they work rather than being placed in a

THE PINWHEEL

nine-to-five position. And 45 percent of millennials will choose workplace flexibility over pay.[18]

Fifty-six percent of millennials won't accept jobs from companies that ban social media.[19] Learn to embrace the social web. Denying millennials today's technology leads to resentment.

Average tenure for millennials is two years, compared to five years for gen Xers and seven years for baby boomers.[20]

To keep millennial talent, rethink your current company culture, and find ways to infuse more flexibility, technology, and socialness. Otherwise, be prepared to pay the price. It costs an average of $24,000 to replace each millennial employee.[21]

But first, just a word of caution. It seems like people research and write about the generations as if everyone in that category fits the characteristics perfectly. The reality is that when we talk about traditionalists, baby boomers, gen Xers, or millennials, the descriptions of wants, needs, and behaviors are averages. They fit the majority but not all of the people in that generational category. As an example, Terry and Steve are baby boomers. However, although there are similarities in work styles between us, there are also differences.

It would be a mistake and unfair to the millennials to treat them as though everything published about them applies to all. Again, the descriptors fit some of them all the time, some part of the time, and for a smaller population, almost not at all.

Remember that each generation is to a large extent the product of their parents and the world they grew up in. Baby boomers exhibit characteristics like frugality, loyalty, convention, and a strong work ethic because their parents came through the Great

Depression and World War II. Steve began talking about and coaching work/life balance in the early 1980s, at a time when most baby boomers believed that work was the most important aspect of their lives.

Gen Xers tend to be independent because they were the product of two working parents, and the concept of "latchkey" kids became the norm in many households.

And the millennial population? First of all, there are a lot of them. According to Gallup, there were seventy-three million born between 1980 and 1996 in the United States. That is a lot of today's workforce!

And what do they want? They want flexible work hours, regular feedback from their supervisors, variety in what they do every day, and development of their skills and knowledge. Although they may be engaged in their work, it is only one aspect of their lives. They do not live to work; they work to live. They value spending time with friends, traveling, staying fit, and eating healthfully. And they desire purpose, purpose in their jobs and purpose in their lives.

We see this last one—purpose—as an incredible opportunity for employers who seize it. To paraphrase what the Dalai Lama said in *The Art of Happiness at Work*, "Some work for job, some for career, but we really want those who have purpose."[22] This generation wants purpose like no other before it, and we believe those companies that help them find that purpose will have a huge competitive advantage.

How different from our generation of baby boomers. We just put our heads down and worked hard, pretty much doing what we were told, performing to the best of our abilities, and hoping it would be recognized by management.

Studies have revealed that millennials are the least engaged generation in the workforce today. The question to be asked and ultimately answered is whether they are the least engaged because it's harder to satisfy them or because employers don't understand them well enough to meet their needs. The result of this is that more employed millennials say they are looking for a different job than any prior generation.

Since the central topic of this book is creating a great customer experience through an engaged workforce, the implications of all this cannot be ignored. The fact that there are seventy-three million millennials, most of whom are and will be in the workforce, has profound implications for companies that understand their success is largely tied to employee engagement and customer experience. Finding ways to engage their millennials will to a great extent determine the success of companies that want to win through providing a consistently great customer experience.

What can you do? Understand and respect the fact that millennials are different from any prior generation of workers. Communicate candidly and often with them, coach rather than manage, spend more time on their positive performance characteristics than the negatives, provide them with variety and challenge in their work, offer them career development and growth opportunities, recognize that they are not defined by their work but by their entire lives, and above all, listen to them. They have a lot to say, and they hold the key to the future success of your enterprise.

Questions for Engagement and Action: Millennials

1. How are your people practices changing to support millennials?

2. How have you bridged the culture between the various age groups, from traditionalists to millennials?

SUMMARY

As we stated in the very beginning, these are our stories. Although training can be perishable if not applied quickly, we hope these stores inspire you to action. But as much as we are excited that our stories inspire, this is not the only purpose.

Our belief is that all seven of these elements or vanes of the Pinwheel are needed to balance your business. However, taking all of them on at one time is unrealistic and could potentially confuse your culture. Each year, the assessment should be used to determine the top three priorities to work on in your annual strategic planning session. (You do have annual strategic planning sessions, right?)

For example, *The Ed Sullivan Show* (a variety show from the 1960s) had an act that highlighted a man with the spinning plates. He was mesmerizing. He continually had to prioritize his act with running from plate to plate. You and your team represent the man with the spinning plates. You have to be on your game!

We really believe with all elements of the Pinwheel, there is no point of destination. The world is changing, the culture is moving, the market is challenging, and customers' needs are instantaneous and personal. And if you get these mostly right, with emphasis on working on your top three gaps annually, you have a great shot at consistency and growth with a great brand and loyal employees and customers.

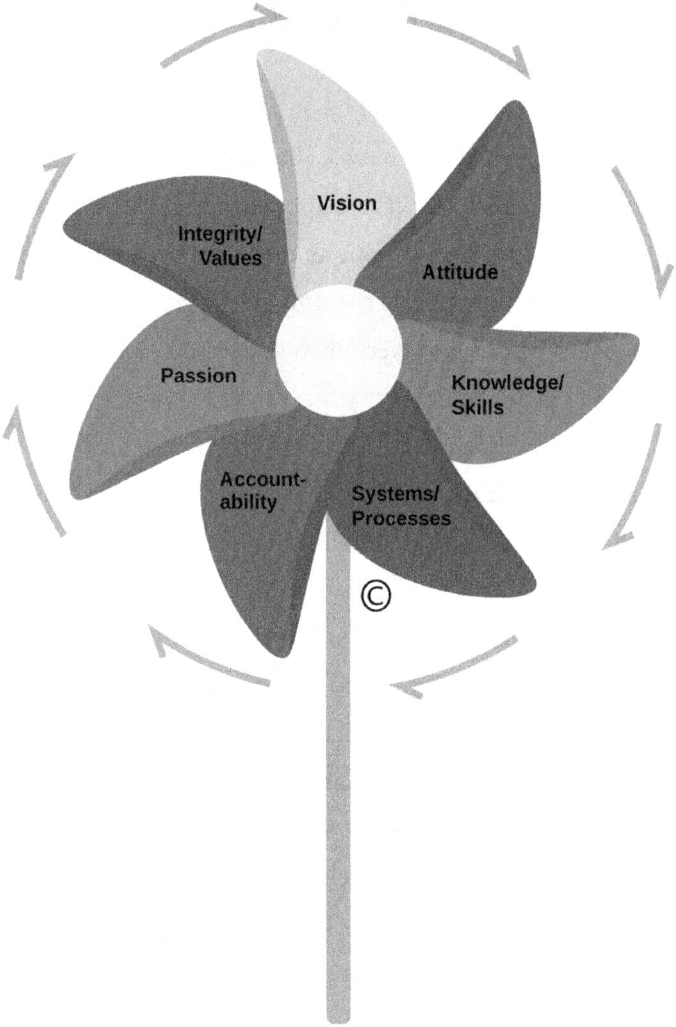
Vision
Attitude
Knowledge/
Skills
Systems/
Processes
Account-
ability
Passion
Integrity/
Values
©

KEY POINTS

Okay, having said that, let's highlight what we believe are some of the key points we covered in the book.

The Pinwheel

We chose this metaphor because it is made up of vanes that spin around a central axis, just as our businesses do. There are seven vanes in our Pinwheel, representing what we believe are the essential components required in building a customer service culture. You will want to conduct an assessment to determine the two or three that you want to tackle first as focus will be critical. Once you have made improvements in those areas, conduct another assessment to determine that next vanes for which improvement is needed. Like a spinning pinwheel, your journey will never be over, so once you have made improvements in all areas, start over again. Remember—your competitors won't be sitting still!

Show Me the Money

We chose this title because we learned through our own experiences that there are some who inherently believe providing great customer experiences is the right thing to do, and there are some who need to understand how it will positively impact the bottom line. Make sure you always have current data at your fingertips for those who need the facts. There is plenty of data out there for those who need to know that the most profitable companies, creating the most shareholder value, are those that have the highest customer satisfaction results.

Vision

The journey begins with a vision of where you want to go. Otherwise, how will you know when you arrive? And when you do arrive, it will be time to establish a new vision. Our experiences have taught us that the most effective visions are created by employees. There are a couple of reasons why this is true. One, employees are the ones who really know what your customers want and need, and how to meet those wants and needs. And second, we all know that people support what they help create. So give them the opportunity to create the vision and see it realized.

Integrity/Values

We believe integrity and values are cornerstones of all we have written about. Why? Because serving customers is all about doing what you say you will do and of meeting commitments or exceeding them. Yes, the story Terry told regarding the "liar" is somewhat hyperbolic, although it wasn't to Terry's wife, who expected him to do what he said he would do. Great companies must be built on a rock of integrity, ethics, and shared values. This applies to great service cultures as well.

Attitude

None of what we have written about will bear much fruit unless you can successfully engage your employees. We love the concept of the service-profit chain, originally created in a Harvard Business School article. It's remarkably simple yet equally brilliant. Engaged employees can deliver great customer experiences, leading to improved shareholder value. Herb Kelleher, to a large extent, built the foundation for Southwest Airlines on this model.

By the way, we have tested this with many groups and classes by having the attendees list the attributes of great customer service. We than ask them to signify whether the attribute is an attitude or a skill. In all cases, the attendees identify around 80 percent of the attributes as attitudes. So most of what comprises great service is attitude, and what kind of employees have great attitudes? You betcha! Engaged employees.

We think using surveys to measure the engagement of your employees is a critical process. But make sure you tell your employees that you heard them and then work alongside them to make the changes they have identified. If you do this at regular intervals, it won't be long before the areas for improvement will be little ones as opposed to the big ones you started with.

Knowledge and Skills

We all know how important effective communication is. How can you consistently meet the wants and needs of your employees or your customers if you don't know what they are?

And remember that effective communication is not only what we say but our ability to effectively listen. We love the "I did not steal your cow today" exercise because it so clearly proves that the words we use are not nearly as important to effective communication as body language, voice inflection, and tone. Spend time with your employees, discussing the dangers of relying too much on e-mails, texts, and other forms of social media that can easily be misunderstood because we cannot see the other person or hear their tones or inflections.

Service Recovery

This is one of our favorite topics because it is so important and yet so often overlooked. We are always surprised when we ask audiences by show of hands how many of them work for companies that have a service recovery process, and few hands go up. No matter how sound your service processes are, there will be times when you let your customers down. But what will you do about it? This is the moment of truth. You have the opportunity to show your customer how much you care and how much integrity is embedded in your culture. Will you prioritize making it right, or put it on the back burner to be dealt with when you have time? And remember—great service recovery builds customer loyalty.

KEY POINTS

Accountability

Don't we want everyone we do business with to be accountable for their words and actions? We told the story that occurred at the Hotel del Coronado as an example of what happens when accountability is demonstrated. Steve went from "I will never do business here again" to "I will not only come back, but I will sing the virtues of this company because of the accountability they demonstrated." If you want to be the leader in your competitive arena, make sure accountability is an integral component of your culture.

Passion

To us, passion is the fuel that ignites the other six elements of the Pinwheel. It is with our hearts that we truly serve. This is why we say that heart + belief = passion. The willingness and commitment to serve come from our hearts, but there must also be a belief that what we are doing is honorable and worthwhile.

Message to Senior Leaders

We added this chapter because we have seen over and over again that significant change occurs when leaders are visible and active, not only in word, but in action. This is why we always want to meet with senior leadership first and assess their willingness and commitment to support the needed changes. Employees want and need to know that leadership truly believes in the initiative being launched and that it's not just the "program of the month."

We tell leaders that if they are not prepared to lead the change from the top, it's best to not take the first step. Your employees will be excited when they learn of the opportunity to create great customer experiences. Don't build their hopes if you are not prepared to see it through to completion.

Millennials

We just couldn't envision a book about employees and customers that didn't include some words regarding the millennials. They are, and will continue to have a major impact on the companies that employ them for the next several years. They are challenging, yes, but that's only because they are not like us. Their motivations, values, and goals are uniquely their own, but that's not bad, just different. So take the time to try to understand what makes them tick, and they will serve you well. As millennials become the dominant generation in the workplace, you have an opportunity through them to lead in customer experience delivery by taking the time to understand and appreciate them.

Finally, remember the insightful words of the Dalai Lama as written in *The Art of Happiness at Work*: We work for job, career, or cause. What is the cause or purpose that you and your employees can get behind so the work is meaningful and worth doing with maximum effort and commitment?

CLOSING

The soft skills presented in chapters 10 and 11 are often overlooked, so we have this for you to think about.

According to *Wikipedia* as of this writing, the English word "enthusiasm" is derived from the Greek *enthousiasmos*, which consists of the root words *theos* (God) and *en* (in).

Thus, "enthusiasm" literally means "God within." We like that. To be enthusiastic is to be inspired or, more precisely, possessed by God.

Doing this work with inspiration and enthusiasm is your calling. It's actually divine. Yes, you will make a living and provide for your teams and customers, but why not be filled with the purpose of doing it right because it's the right thing to do?

It's pretty hard to say no to someone who has connected their beliefs and their actions. It flows into the culture with power and strength, and it creates enthusiasts who are released to find new and innovative ways to serve your customers and improve your financial performance. We wish you the very best experience in your divine work!

ABOUT THE AUTHORS

Pinwheel Partners LLC specializes in coaching and training leadership teams on seven elements that make up a winning culture. The thought leadership from Terry Cain and Steve Church is heavily influenced by 15 years of applying new knowledge that comes each season via the ASU Center for Services Leadership Symposium, as well as extensive experience in the Fortune 500 marketplace. Now the principals at Pinwheel Partners, both Steve and Terry have been regular faculty at the Annual CSL Symposium, The Services Leadership Institute, as well as guest faculty in undergraduate and MBA classes. They both are Emeritus board members of WP Carey Center for Services Leadership and enjoy the interaction of students, as well as participating in business events and conferences of all sizes. Teamed together, they make the experience lively and unique for all audiences.

THE PINWHEEL

Steve Church

After leading the most profitable north American business unit as president, Steve was instrumental in starting the services business models within Avnet. He held positions as Vice President of Corporate Marketing, Chief Human Resources Officer, Corporate Strategy Officer, Corporate Business Development Officer, and Chief Operational Excellence Officer. His leadership drove global commitment to Avnet's core values that was foundational to the growth of the company during a period of numerous acquisitions, driving consistency in the employee experience for all.

Steve lives in Phoenix, Arizona, and enjoys spending time with his three adult children and three grandchildren.

ABOUT THE AUTHORS

Terry Cain

Terry is passionate about building a business culture that serves with excellence. His experience includes 30 Years in Fortune 500, Sales, Business Development, Process Mastery, Change Management and Customer Engagement.

After leading regional sales businesses within Avnet, Terry discovered a strong skillset and passion for starting new business development and strategies. Then as Vice President of Shared Business Services and Vice President of Global Operational Excellence, Terry drove change management, and employee led process improvement. His "dream position" as Vice President responsible for Global Customer Engagement led to the co-writing of the book, *The Pinwheel*. Terry has numerous guest lecturer/speaker appearances including Kellogg at Northwestern, Eller at University of Arizona, Argyle Leadership Events, Richmond events, NG Customer Experience and many others all focused on Customer culture.

Terry lives in Phoenix, Arizona with his wife Rebecca, and enjoys time with his son and new daughter-in-law.

ENDNOTES

Avnet

Avnet, Inc., is a business-to-business technology distributor headquartered in Phoenix, Arizona. Avnet is a Fortune 500 company and one of the largest global distributors of electronic components, computer products, and embedded technology.

1. Smith, D. (July 2004). We, Incorporated. *Fast Company*.
2. Anderson, K., R. Zemke (1998). *Delivering Knock Your Socks Off Service*. New York: AMACOM.
3. Hammer, M., & J. Champy (1993). *Reengineering the Corporation: A Manifesto for Business Revolution*. New York: HarperCollins.
4. Wikipedia.org, the Free Encyclopedia.
5. Anders, G. (March 27, 2016). "Did Peter Drucker actually say 'culture eats strategy for breakfast'—and if so, where/when?" Retrieved from www.quora.com/Did-Peter-Drucker-actually-say-culture-eats-strategy-for-breakfast-and-if-so-where-when.
6. Zenger, J., & J. Folkman (March 2013). "The ideal praise-to-criticism ratio." Retrieved from https://hbr.org/2013/03/the-ideal-praise-to-criticism.
7. Ko, V. (April 14, 2013). "Can you cope with criticism at work?" Retrieved from http://www.cnn.com/2013/04/14/business/criticism-praise-feedback-work-life/.

[8] A. Krishna, G. Dangayach, & S. Sharma, "Service recovery paradox: The success parameters," *Global Business Review* 15, no. 2 (2014): 263–277.
[9] Sons of Maxwell, (2009, July 06). United Breaks Guitars. Retrieved from https://www.youtube.com/watch?v=5YGc4zOqozo
[10] Deighton, John A., & Leora Kornfeld, "United Breaks Guitars." Harvard Business School Case 510-057, January 2010. (Revised August 2011.)
[11] NNEVPCliff, (2011, February 19). Johnny the Bagger. Retrieved from https://www.youtube.com/watch?v=IQlxLBqgFKc
[12] DiFranco, T. (2012, November 30). The Death Crawl scene from Facing the Giants. Retrieved from https://www.youtube.com/watch?v=-sUKoKQlEC4&t=8s
[13] Katdangers. (2011, April 19). Thumbs Up for Rock and Roll! Retrieved from https://www.youtube.com/watch?v=eaIvk1cSyG8
[14] www.brainyquote.com.
[15] For a deeper dive into ADKAR, see https://www.prosci.com.
[16] Gallup, I. (2016). "How millennials want to work and live. Retrieved from http://www.gallup.com/reports/189830/millennials-work-live.aspx.
[17] Schawbel, D. (March 29, 2012). "Millennials vs. baby boomers: Who would you rather hire?" Retrieved from http://business.time.com/2012/03/29/millennials-vs-baby-boomers-who-would-you-rather-hire/.
[18] Schawbel, D. (October 29, 2014). "Hiring managers say millennials surpass prior generations in several key business skills, new study reveals." Retrieved from https://www.upwork.com/press/2014/10/29/hiring-managers-say-millennials-surpass-prior-generations-in-several-key-business-skills-new-study-reveals-2/.
[19] Schawbel, D. (June 25, 2013). "74 of the most interesting facts about millennials." Retrieved from http://danschawbel.com/blog/74-of-the-most-interesting-facts-about-the-millennial-generation/.
[20] Schawbel, D. (August 6, 2013). "Millennial Branding and Beyond. com survey reveals the rising cost of hiring workers from the

millennial generation." Retrieved from http://millennialbranding. com/category/blog.
[21] Ibid.
[22] Lama, D., and H. C. Cutler (2003). *The Art of Happiness at Work.* New York: Riverhead Books.

ACKNOWLEDGMENTS

Our book has been in the making for more than fifteen years. We have had the privilege of working with and observing many people who have influenced and inspired us during that time.

First, the repeated exposure to thought leadership, innovations, and best practices would not have been possible without the WP Carey Center for Services Leadership (CSL). There are many at the center to thank, but we would like to particularly mention executive directors Dr. Stephen Brown, Mary Jo Bitner, and Wolfgang Ulaga; Dean Amy Hillman; and Professors Nancy Stephens, Amy Ostrom, and Douglas Olsen. Also, the director of business partnerships, Alicia Holder.

The spirit of our book has to a large extent been created by our friends at the Center for Services Leadership. Their encouragement and inclusion in their classrooms to test out new thoughts and ways of teaching, as well as the opportunity to bounce ideas off the great minds of the MBA students, has been priceless. This is where we met the member companies that make up the center, also significantly shaping our body of learning. These are great companies like Cox, Intel, Schwab, Abbott Labs, Honeywell, and Cardinal Health. We have had many heart-to-heart conversations with the members and shared our experiences, speaking to each other's teams large and small.

Another rewarding part of this journey. Thank you, David Ridley, formerly of Southwest Airlines, as well as Bernie Clark of Schwab, Adrian Paull of Honeywell, Lee Scalzano at Cox, Michelle Proctor of FedEx, Ed Petrozelli and Tom Esposito from the Insight Group, and Bobbie Dangerfield from Dell for your openness and sharing. You make a difference!

We would also like to acknowledge some of the speakers and teachers not mentioned in the book, including Frederick Reichheld, Bain and Co.; Colin Shaw, Beyond Philosophy; Jeanne Bliss, Customer Bliss; Bruce Temkin, Temkin Group; Jim Hauden, Gary Magenta, and David Kalman, all at Root Inc.; Joe Wheeler, The Service Profit Chain Institute; and Stan Phelps, The Purple Goldfish. These thought leaders took our calls or met with us and offered guiding encouragement. Thank you!

We also need to thank Avnet, Inc., the company we were blessed to spend most of our careers with and where we had the opportunity to teach and learn. Avnet's innovative model for training leaders, one we referred to as "leaders teaching leaders" in small-group settings, had a large influence on what and how we have taught.

Thanks also to Patrick McAvoy from Sierra Marketing, long-term friend and consultant for your insightful engagement and great tools, always. To our graphic artist, Derek Brennan, thank you for helping us add a little fun, for your work on the Pinwheel colors, and 100 percent of the artwork in the book. And to Marilou Nobley, Terry's sister, who gave of her time to help us stay on track as we moved through the structure and flow of

ACKNOWLEDGMENTS

writing. Thank you for your patience, care, and love for us and the project, and your great questions.

A big sincere "thank you" goes to the endorsees of our book, who are friends, colleagues, and mentors. We fully realize that endorsing someone or something is a form of making a referral. When we endorse or refer someone, we put our reputations on the line. We are grateful and humbled that the following august group would be willing to endorse our work.

Ann Rhoades: Your vision and care for employees at Southwest Airlines were likely the first inspiration for what a business can be, starting with the right people and proving it to the world.

To our friends at Globoforce: Eric Mosley, CEO, your inspiration and continual gift of thanks to your employees is an example of a company that walks the talk of culture and employee engagement. Thanks to Derek Irvine for being a constant light and energy for teaching your customers *The Power of Thanks* (book). I have to thank Brian Miele for the best service recovery possible in those early days!

Chris Zane, CEO, Zane's Cycles, author of *Reinventing the Wheel: The Science of Creating Lifetime Customers*, whose customer focus started when he bought his first bike shop at age fifteen! Your stories live on!

Adrian Paull, SVP, Honeywell, for your constant challenging and great examples of leading a culture that created, and includes, customer council best practices.

Ed Petrozelli, president, Insight Group, who along with Tom Esposito have consistently provided thought leadership to companies needing to add services and solutions to their offerings.

Dr. Stephen Brown, for your vision for the Center for Services Leadership and providing a great platform for businesses to grow in knowledge and skills. And Mary Jo Bitner, who along with Stephen Brown coauthored the book *Profiting from Services and Solutions: What Product-Centric Firms Need to Know*, and who is also the author of our foreword.

Carine Clark, president and CEO at Go Banyan, Inc., who showed relentless commitment to meet the needs of customers when things get tough.

Terry Speaking

Thank you, dear Becky; our son, Jon, and his wife-to-be, Katie; all of you encourage me with your ideas, love, and hope. Mark Twain said he could live two months on a good compliment; with this team behind me, I will be pushing a hundred for sure!

Thank you, Dad—Louie B. Cain—pastor, teacher, student, tinkerer, whimsical thinker, and dreamer. One of his tenets is "Do as much as you can, but don't force it!" We all know when we are forcing something! This has become a basic truth in this work, as in all work. I remember working a jigsaw puzzle with Dad when I was about eight years old. Losing patience with the process, I jammed a piece into the puzzle. It was the right color and the right shape, but the blunt edges on all sides clearly showed that I had forced it into the spot. Dad looked at my effort and asked, "Does that one fit?" I want to thank Dad for his ability to gently put us in place, without forcing.

I want to thank Steve Church for encouraging me in our

work from the very beginning. When working directly for him, it was a joy to keep focused in a corporate world designed to keep us all "forced," off balance, and unfocused. As Tom Rath wrote in the book *Vital Friends*, research has revealed the importance of friendship and trust in the workplace that increases productivity and results. Steve, thanks for being one of my vital friends.

Steve Speaking

I would like to thank Roy Vallee, former CEO of Avnet, who gave me so many of the opportunities that have shaped my career. I want to thank my children—Kimberly, Jessica, and Dan—and my grandchildren—Bear, RubySue, and Levi—who remind me often about what's really important in life. And my parents, who demonstrated by example how hard work and a desire to be the best at whatever we do in life is what's important.

I would like to thank the small group of companies that have provided me with great customer experiences, proving that it can be done and done consistently. I would also like to thank those who have provided disappointing experiences, as there is as much or more to learn from bad experiences than from good ones.

I would finally like to thank Terry Cain for his friendship and patience as we have worked through the writing of this book and the creation of our business model. There are few things in life more rewarding than having a friend who is also your business partner.

THE PINWHEEL

From Both

Last and most important, we thank our God and Father, His Son Jesus Christ, and the Holy Spirit. Every breath we take is on purpose, and we are held together by His love and grace.

Terry **Steve**

Open Book Editions
A Berrett-Koehler Partner

Open Book Editions is a joint venture between Berrett-Koehler Publishers and Author Solutions, the market leader in self-publishing. There are many more aspiring authors who share Berrett-Koehler's mission than we can sustainably publish. To serve these authors, Open Book Editions offers a comprehensive self-publishing opportunity.

A Shared Mission

Open Book Editions welcomes authors who share the Berrett-Koehler mission—Creating a World That Works for All. We believe that to truly create a better world, action is needed at all levels—individual, organizational, and societal. At the individual level, our publications help people align their lives with their values and with their aspirations for a better world. At the organizational level, we promote progressive leadership and management practices, socially responsible approaches to business, and humane and effective organizations. At the societal level, we publish content that advances social and economic justice, shared prosperity, sustainability, and new solutions to national and global issues.

Open Book Editions represents a new way to further the BK mission and expand our community. We look forward to helping more authors challenge conventional thinking, introduce new ideas, and foster positive change.

For more information, see the Open Book Editions website: http://www.iuniverse.com/Packages/OpenBookEditions.aspx

Join the BK Community! See exclusive author videos, join discussion groups, find out about upcoming events, read author blogs, and much more! http://bkcommunity.com/

Printed in the United States
By Bookmasters